I hope...

Moments of love, accountability,
and thoughtfulness

ISBN: 9798349314490

"Therefore, since we have been justified through faith, we have peace with God through our Lord Jesus Christ, through whom we have gained access by faith into this grace in which we now stand. And we boast in the hope of the glory of God. Not only so, but we also glory in our sufferings, because we know that suffering produces perseverance; perseverance, character; and character, hope. And hope does not put us to shame, because God's love has been poured out into our hearts through the Holy Spirit, who has been given to us."
Romans 5:1-5 NIV

-Foreword-

I struggle with the concept of explaining. When is it necessary? When is it too much? So when it comes to "I hope..." this is no different but I'm going to attempt to find the balance.

I received peace and confirmation from God that I would have a published book before the year is over. I trusted Him for another book series I was writing because this right here was not even thought of, by me, in that moment. But He always knows.

I am often told by my friends that I need to put my positivity and encouragement in a book. One week I decided to spend quiet time with God and have Him guide me. Thus, "I hope..." was written.

-Foreword-

This book truly comes from moments of love, accountability, and thoughtfulness in platonic dealings with friends and family, intimacy with a loved one, and quiet time with self.

Overall, the moments provided are for you to interpret for the space you're in right now. Some moments may not relate to you and that is fine, don't force an understanding. Simply pass those on to someone who may find it beneficial. But if you have a moment that causes you to pause and ponder, grab a journal and explore those thoughts.

This book is to serve as a reminder and push to be gentle with yourself as we pinpoint and acknowledge the areas of our life that are not okay to allow for growth and healing.

I hope...

you read this and are able to connect with it
mentally, spiritually, and emotionally
no matter where you are on life's journey.
I pray it encourages you to be your best in all ways.

With love and gratefulness,
Leah Đavis

I hope your effort and growth
remain intact without the validation
or acknowledgement of others.

I hope you stand strong in what you know even when you can't see it.

I hope you let those rebuttals from
made up arguments go.

I hope you forgive yourself for that
embarrassment that happened
ten years ago.
A year ago.
A week ago.
A day ago.

I hope you accept the
annoying things you do that make
you human.

I hope your supportive words are
followed through by
supportive action.

I hope you don't allow
someone else's success to
diminish your own.

I hope you let go of the promises
you made in failed relationships
to allow you, and them, to grow.

I hope the "other person" you choose to obsess over is actually the one you should be worried about.

'I hope you practice love and kindness everyday; not only when it's convenient for you.

I hope you forgive that person before you realize you, too, are in need of forgiveness.

I hope you think before you speak
understanding that your tongue has
equal power in
destroying and encouraging.

I hope you humble yourself before
it's too late.

I hope your freedom doesn't come at
the expense of someone's pain.

I hope you get over the point you're
trying to prove;
feel you have to prove.

I hope you allow others to grow
beyond what you've previously
thought of them.

I hope you trust what you know.

'I hope you don't allow feelings to
rule your life.

I hope you don't force it.

I hope you don't let your
environment dictate your mood or
sway your magnetic energy.

I hope you follow through.

I hope you use your faith in God as a
power move.

I hope you don't use your kindness
or apologies as manipulation to
maintain power.

I hope you humble yourself.

I hope you acknowledge your
wrongs or shortcomings.

I hope you receive His peace.

I hope you allow others to
think and act
beyond your limited thoughts.

I hope you find your safe space.

I hope you don't allow your
mistakes and fears to cripple you.

I hope you know that's
not your only story.

I hope you own it.

I hope you are present.

I hope you love without inhibitions;
romantically and platonically.

I hope you are always
willing and open to learn.

I hope you aren't afraid to live.

I hope you realize rejection is not the
final say and there is a
beautiful lesson in the midst of it.

I hope you detach from self and
see the bigger picture.

I hope you stay committed to the
gifts that make you, you.

I hope you stay inspired.

I hope you pray to cover the
generations after you.

I hope you learn the difference between venting and talking behind someone's back; if there is one.

I hope you learn to communicate your
feelings properly,
before the moment passes.

I hope you learn how to truly be still.

I hope you realize
how powerful you are.

I hope you don't allow your
overthinking to cloud
God's promises for you.

I hope you listen.

I hope you learn that just because
you know what "it" is doesn't mean
you know how to deal with "it;"
seek help.

I hope you pinpoint the areas in your life where you've self sabotaged and stop that behavior in its tracks.

I hope you remember it's your life.
Don't be afraid to live it.

I hope you know you are loved.